PRIMARY SOURCES OF AMERICAN WARS™

The Mexican-American War

Georgene Poulakidas

The Rosen Publishing Group's
PowerKids Press™
PRIMARY SOURCE

For my brother Dean

Published in 2006 by The Rosen Publishing Group, Inc.
29 East 21st Street, New York, NY 10010

First Edition

Editor: Eric Fein
Book Design: Erica Clendening
Photo Researcher: Peter Tomlinson

Photo Credits: Cover, pp. 8 (right), 10 (right), 12, 14 (right), 16 (bottom), 18 (bottom) Library of Congress Prints and Photographs Division; pp. 4, 20 (bottom) Library of Congress, Geography and Map Division; p. 6 (left) © Getty Images; p. 6 (right) © New-York Historical Society, New York, USA/Bridgeman Art Library; p. 8 (left) Broadsides Collections, Earl Vandale Collection, Center for American History, University of Texas at Austin; p. 10 (left) Library of Congress, Rare Book and Special Collections Division; p. 14 (left) Society of California Pioneers, San Francisco; p. 16 (top) Courtesy Texas State Archives Map Collection; p. 18 (top) Picture Collection, The Branch Libraries, The New York Public Library, Astor, Lenox, and Tilden Foundations; p. 20 (top) National Archives and Records Administration, General Records of the United States Government, Record Group 11.

Library of Congress Cataloging-in-Publication Data

Poulakidas, Georgene.
    The Mexican-American War / Georgene Poulakidas.— 1st ed.
    p. cm. — (Primary sources of American wars)
    Includes index
    ISBN 1-4042-2683-4 (lib. bdg.)
    1. Mexican War, 1846–1848—Juvenile literature. I. Title. II. Series.

E404.P68 2006
973.6'2—dc22

                                                          2003028040

Manufactured in the United States of America

Contents

Map of the
UNITED STATES
OF
NORTH AMERICA
With parts of the Adjacent Countries.
BY
David H. Burr

4

The Causes of War

The Mexican-American War, fought between 1846 and 1848, was the result of many disagreements between the United States and Mexico. Two of the main causes of the war were the **annexation** of Texas into the United States and the disagreement over the location of the Texas-Mexico border. These problems were caused largely by the westward movement of American settlers into Mexican **territories**.

The settlers had moved into the Mexican territories to start new lives. They were obtaining land to farm, establishing businesses, and coming to trade or hunt. However, as time passed, the Mexican government became unhappy that such large numbers of Americans were living in their territories.

■ *This 1839 map shows the United States and Mexico (the large area on the left, outlined in yellow). By this time, thousands of American settlers were living in Mexican territory.*

Stephen Austin (1793–1836, above) is often called the Father of Texas. Austin was the commander of the volunteer army that fought for Texas independence. The state capital of Texas—Austin—is named for him.

Mexico's Trouble in Texas

By the 1830s, thousands of settlers from the United States had come to Texas. At the time, Texas was controlled by Mexico. However, these Americans were angered by Mexico's attempts to refuse to allow Texas to govern itself. They were also opposed to Mexico's laws, which attempted to slow down the flow of Americans into Texas.

During this time, Mexico was having problems keeping civil order. In 1833, General Santa Anna was elected president of Mexico. About a year later, Santa Anna seized total control of Mexico, becoming its **dictator**. The American settlers thought that Santa Anna would deal with them fairly, but he did not. When Stephen Austin, the leader of the settlers, advised the settlers to set up their own government, the Mexicans sent him to jail. This angered the settlers. Fighting soon broke out between the settlers and the Mexican soldiers.

■ *Antonio Lopez de Santa Anna (1794–1876, left) was a military man and the president of Mexico on five different occasions. He is said to have been a very good leader, but he was not skilled at running the government of Mexico.*

7

■ The Texas Declaration of Independence (left) was made on March 2, 1836. In it, American settlers living under Mexican control announced their freedom and their desire to establish their own independent republic.

8

The Texas Revolution

In 1835, Santa Anna sent more soldiers to Texas to stop the fighting. The settlers **revolted** and established Texas as an independent **republic**. The first battle of the Texas Revolution was fought in October 1835. In February 1836, the Battle of the Alamo was fought. The Alamo was a fort in San Antonio, Texas. For 13 days, about 200 Texans, led by William Travis and Davy Crockett, held off Santa Anna's force of about 5,000 men. In the end, however, all the American soldiers were killed. Yet, the Texans continued their fight. In April 1836, they defeated Mexican forces at the Battle of San Jacinto, the final fight of the **revolution**. However, Mexico refused to accept Texas as an independent republic and warned the United States not to make Texas a state.

■ *This painting, created in about 1912, shows the Battle of the Alamo in February 1836. The deaths of the Americans who defended the fort inspired the battle cry, "Remember the Alamo!" Texas soldiers shouted this at their victory at the Battle of San Jacinto, which brought Texas its independence.*

NO ANNEXATION

OF

TEXAS

It having been announced by the Government organ that a Treaty for the Annexation of Texas has been negociated and signed, and will soon be presented to the Senate, the undersigned call upon the citizens of New York, without distinction of Party, who are opposed to the Ratification of said Treaty, to meet at the Tabernacle, on Monday evening, the 22d of April inst., to express their opposition to the same.

Dated, New York, April 18th, 1844.

■ Not all Americans believed that Texas should become part of the United States. This flyer was made in New York in 1844. It urged citizens to oppose the annexation of Texas into the United States.

On the Border of Danger

In 1845, the U.S. Congress approved the annexation of Texas to the United States. Mexico was so angered that it broke its **diplomatic** ties with the United States. However, U.S. president James Polk sent James Slidell, a government official, to Mexico to **negotiate** a peaceful solution to the problem. Slidell offered to pay Mexico for the loss of Texas. Slidell also had instructions to try to buy California and New Mexico from the Mexican government. Mexico refused and sent troops to the Rio Grande River.

The annexation of Texas caused further disagreements between the two countries. Mexico **claimed** that the border between Texas and the United States was the Nueces River. However, the United States insisted that the border was the Rio Grande River, 150 miles (241 km) south of the Nueces.

■ *John Slidell (1793–1871) was a lawyer and politician. From 1845 to 1846, he was the U.S. minister to Mexico. Slidell worked to find a peaceful solution to the tensions between the United States and Mexico.*

Zachary Taylor (1784–1850, left) was a war hero of the Mexican-American War. He won important battles at Buena Vista and Monterrey, Mexico. Taylor's nickname was Old Rough and Ready. In 1848, he was elected president of the United States.

War!

In April 1846, under orders from President Polk, Major General Zachary Taylor led about 4,000 U.S. soldiers toward the Rio Grande. On April 25, Mexican soldiers attacked a small group of Taylor's soldiers, north of the Rio Grande. When Polk heard of the attack, he asked the U.S. Congress to **declare** war on Mexico. Polk told Congress that Mexico had spilled American blood on American land. Most members of Congress believed that the United States would gain much land if it won a war.

Even before war was officially declared on May 13, Taylor's troops fought Mexican soldiers in two important battles. On May 8 and 9, Taylor's forces defeated Mexican troops led by General Mariano Arista. These back-to-back victories allowed Taylor's forces to cross the Rio Grande and enter Mexico.

■ *This painting of the Battle of Palo Alto was made in 1846. Days after General Taylor won the battle against Mexican soldiers, the United States officially declared war against Mexico.*

This flag was raised to celebrate the Americans' victory when U.S. colonel John C. Fremont captured a Mexican fort at Fort Sonoma in California. It is known as the California Bear Flag. The flag was destroyed in an earthquake in San Francisco in 1906.

JOHN C. FREMONT.

Entered according to act of Congress in the year 1861 by L. Prang & Co.
in the Clerks Office of the District Court of Massachusetts.
Pub.d & Lith.d by L. Prang & Co. Boston.
J. Raven, Sole Agent, 31 Exchange St.

The United States Strikes Fast

Once the war officially started, the United States moved quickly. In June 1846, General Stephen Kearny led 1,700 troops from Fort Leavenworth, Kansas, to New Mexico. By August 1846, Kearny's forces reached Santa Fe, New Mexico, and took control of it. From there, he set out to take California.

In June 1846, Colonel John C. Fremont also led a revolt by American settlers against Mexican rule in California—even before news of the war had reached them. Fremont's forces captured a fort at Sonoma, north of San Francisco. They declared California the Bear Flag Republic. However, on July 7, 1846, U.S. naval forces along the Pacific Coast ordered the U.S. flag raised at nearby Monterey. California had now been officially claimed by the United States government, rather than by American settlers.

■ *John C. Fremont (1813–1890) was a mapmaker and explorer of the American West. He was named military governor of California for his victory at Sonoma. Fremont later struck it rich during the California gold rush, becoming a multimillionaire.*

This drawing is a bird's-eye view of the Battle of Buena Vista, fought in February 1847. It shows the positions of American and Mexican troops and land features such as mountains and gullies.

16

The Battles of Buena Vista and Veracruz

On February 22 to 23, 1847, the Battle of Buena Vista was fought near Monterrey, Mexico. In the Battle of Buena Vista, General Taylor's force of 5,000 soldiers defended a mountain **pass** against Mexican forces that numbered about 20,000 men. The Mexicans were led by General Santa Anna. By winning this battle, the U.S. forces were able to establish their hold on northeastern Mexico.

In March 1847, U.S. general Winfield Scott and a force of about 10,000 men attacked the town of Veracruz, New Mexico. Scott's forces fired about 6,700 shells at the city. In addition to the Mexican soldiers, many Mexican citizens were also killed. After two days of fighting, Scott's troops gained control of the town. When Santa Anna heard about the fall of Veracruz, he immediately set out to stop the Americans from advancing further into Mexico.

■ *In this print, leaders of the Mexican army are shown surrendering their arms to U.S. general Winfield Scott after the battle at Veracruz. In the background, Mexican troops are shown leaving the city.*

This illustration (left) shows American forces marching into Mexico City, the capital of Mexico. By gaining control of the city, the United States had officially won the war.

The Battle of Cerro Gordo and the Fall of Mexico City

On April 17 to 18, 1847, U.S. forces fought the Battle of Cerro Gordo. Cerro Gordo was a mountain pass northwest of Veracruz. Winfield Scott led about 9,000 men in an attack against Santa Anna's forces, which numbered about 13,000 men. The Americans forced the Mexican troops to withdraw.

On August 20, 1847, Scott's forces won the Battle of Churubusco. Churubusco was a town south of Mexico City. Scott had only 9,000 men to oppose Mexico's 30,000 troops. However, the Americans had better equipment and leaders. The Mexican troops were forced to seek shelter behind the walls of Mexico City.

The American **victory** at the Battle of Chapultepec brought the war to an end. This battle was fought near the gates to Mexico City on September 12, 1847. The Americans had gained control of Mexico City, the home of the Mexican government.

■ *This painting (left) is of the Battle of Churubusco, fought in August 1847. In the battle, General Scott's greatly outnumbered troops defeated the Mexican army.*

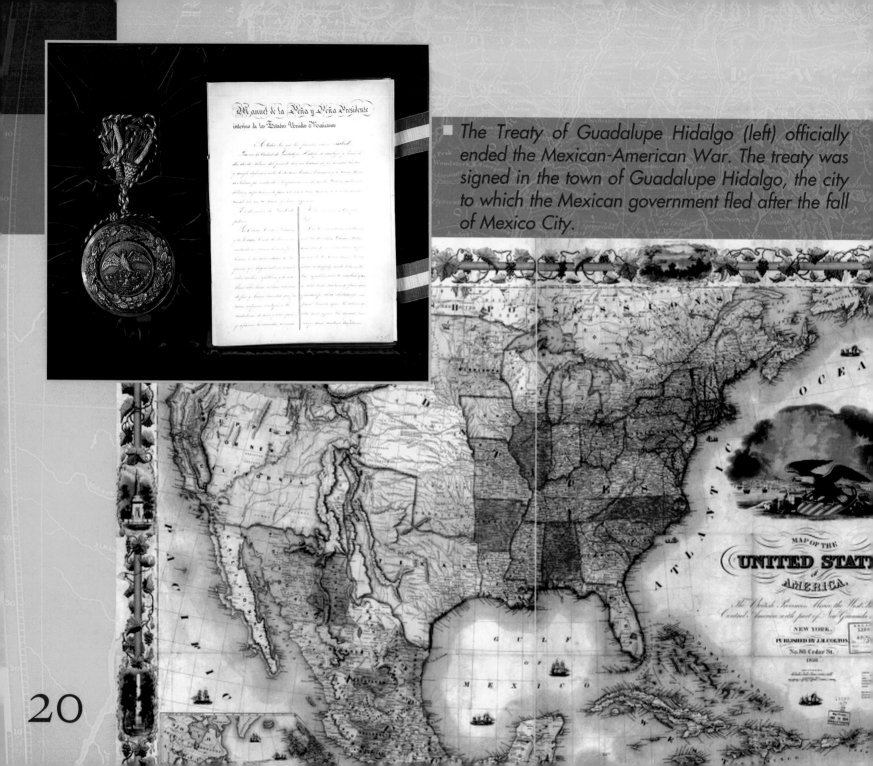

The Treaty of Guadalupe Hidalgo (left) officially ended the Mexican-American War. The treaty was signed in the town of Guadalupe Hidalgo, the city to which the Mexican government fled after the fall of Mexico City.

20

Paying for Peace

Even before the war ended, President Polk had sent Nicholas Trist to Mexico to work out a peace **treaty** between the two warring nations. After months of hard work, Trist was able to get the Mexican government to agree to the Treaty of Guadalupe Hidalgo, which was signed on February 2, 1848.

The treaty set the southern **boundary** of Texas at the Rio Grande River. Mexico was forced to give up New Mexico, California, and all claims to Texas. Mexico also gave up territory that would later become the states of Arizona, Nevada, and Utah, as well as parts of Kansas, Oklahoma, Colorado, and Wyoming. In return, the United States paid Mexico $15 million and settled claims that some Americans had against Mexico. However, bitter feelings would remain on both sides for years to come.

■ *Mexico gave up 55 percent of its territory to the United States in the Treaty of Guadalupe Hidalgo. The map shows the Mexican land in the west and southwest of America that became part of the United States.*

Timeline

Early 1800s	Thousands of American settlers move to Texas.
1833	General Santa Anna is elected president of Mexico.
Early 1830s	Fighting occurs between Texas settlers and Mexican soldiers.
1835–1836	The Texas Revolution is fought. Texas wins and becomes an independent republic.
1845	Texas is annexed to the United States. Disagreements over the Texas boundary begin.
April 1846	Major General Zachary Taylor leads about 4,000 soldiers to the Rio Grande River. Fighting develops between Mexican soldiers and Taylor's men.
May 8–9 1846	Before war is officially declared, Taylor and his troops engage Mexico in two important battles.
May 13, 1846	The United States officially declares war on Mexico.
June 1846	Colonel John C. Fremont leads American settlers in battle against the Mexican government in California.
August 1846	U.S. forces, led by General Stephen Kearny, capture New Mexico.
February 22–23, 1847	The Battle of Buena Vista is fought.
March 1847	The Battle of Veracruz is fought.
April 17–18, 1847	The Battle of Cerro Gordo is fought.
August 20, 1847	The Battle of Churubusco is fought.
September 12, 1847	The Battle of Chapultepec is fought, bringing to an end the fighting between Mexico and the United States.
February 2, 1848	The Treaty of Guadalupe Hidalgo is signed, officially ending the war.

Glossary

annexation (an-EKS-zay-shuhn) When a country adds the land or territory of another country to its own land in order to create a larger nation.

boundary (BOUN-duh-ree) The line, fence, etc., that separates one area from another.

claimed (KLAYMD) To have said something belongs to you or that you had a right to have it.

declare (di-KLAIR) To announce something formally.

dictator (DIK-tay-tur) Someone who has complete control of a country, often ruling it unjustly.

diplomatic (DIP-luh-mat-ik) Having to do with the representation of one country's government in a foreign country.

negotiate (ni-GOH-shee-ate) To bargain or discuss something so that you can come to an agreement.

pass (PASS) A narrow passage in a mountain range.

republic (ri-PUHB-lik) A country that has a form of government in which the people have the power to elect representatives who manage the government. Republics often have presidents.

revolted (ri-VOHLT-ihd) To have fought against authority.

revolution (rev-uh-LOO-shuhn) A violent uprising by people of a country that changes its system of government.

territories (TER-uh-tor-eez) The land and waters under the control of a state, nation, or ruler.

treaty (TREE-tee) A formal agreement between two or more countries.

victory (VIK-tuh-ree) A win in a battle or contest.

Index

Primary Sources

Cover: *Attack on the Castle Chapultepec.* Hand-colored lithograph by Currier & Ives [1848]. Library of Congress Prints and Photographs Division. **Page 4:** *Map of the United States of North America with parts of the adjacent countries.* Created by David H. Burr, geographer to the House of Representatives of the United States [1839]. Library of Congress Geography and Map Division. **Page 6 (left):** Drawing of Stephen F. Austin [c. 1820]. Artist unknown. **Page 6 (right):** Portrait of Antonio Lopez de Santa Anna by Paul L'Ouvrier. Oil on linen [c. 1858]. **Page 8 (inset):** Texas Declaration of Independence, Original Manuscript, March 2, 1836. Texas State Library & Archives Commission. **Page 8:** *Battle of the Alamo.* Painting by Percy Moran [c. 1912]. Library of Congress Prints and Photographs Division. **Page 10 (inset):** "No Annexation of Texas." Original broadside [1844]. Library of Congress Printed Ephemera Collection. **Page 10:** Photo of John Slidell [c. 1860–1865]. National Archives at College Park. **Page 12 (inset):** *Major General Zachary Taylor: "Rough & Ready."* Hand-colored lithograph by Currier & Ives [c. 1847]. Library of Congress Prints and Photographs Division. **Page 12:** *Battle of Palo Alto.* Hand-colored lithograph by E. B. & E. C. Kellogg [1846]. Library of Congress Prints and Photographs Division. **Page 14 (inset):** The California Bear Flag. Society of California Pioneers. **Page 14:** *John C. Fremont/Fabronius.* Lithograph by L. Prang & Co. [1861]. Library of Congress Prints and Photographs Division. **Page 16 (inset):** *A Key to the Battle of Buena Vista* [c. 1847]. Texas State Library and Archives Commission. **Page 16:** *The Mexicans evacuating Vera Cruz, and surrendering their arms to the U.S. Army, under Genl. Scott.* Hand-colored lithograph by Sarony & Major [c. 1847]. Library of Congress Prints and Photographs Division. **Page 18 (inset):** *The Occupation of the capital of Mexico by the American army.* Painting by Christian Schussele [1847]. Print Collection, Miriam and Ira D. Wallach Division of Art, Prints, and Photographs, New York Public Library, Astor, Lenox, and Tilden Foundations. **Page 18:** *Battle of Churubusco—Fought near the city of Mexico 20th of August 1847.* Hand-colored lithograph by Currier & Ives. J. Cameron, artist. **Page 20 (inset):** Treaty of Guadalupe Hidalgo [1848]. National Archives and Records Administration. **Page 20:** *Map of the United States of America.* Created by J. H. Colton and Company [1857]. Library of Congress Geography and Map Division.

Web Sites

Due to the changing nature of Internet links, PowerKids Press has developed an online list of Web sites related to the topic of this book. This site is updated regularly. Please use this link to access the list:
http://www.powerkidslinks.com/psaw/maw/